Best of British

Brian Glover

First published in 1998 for
Tesco Stores Limited
by Brilliant Books Ltd
84-86 Regent Street
London W1R 6DD

Origination by Colourpath Ltd, London
Printed and bound by Jarrold Book Printing,
Thetford, England

Best of British

Brian Glover

TESCO

About the author

Brian Glover was named the 1997 Magazine Food Writer of the Year by the Guild of Food Writers and regularly contributes to *Tesco Recipe Magazine* and *Homes & Gardens*. He was raised on a farm in Lancashire, but has since lived in Liverpool, Yorkshire, Devon and London. He loves British food.

Photographer   Peter Cassidy

Home economist   Bridget Sargeson

Stylist   Roisin Nield

Recipes tested by Jacqueline Bellefontaine

                       Terry Farris

CONTENTS

INTRODUCTION

The recipes in this book have been created and photographed specially for Tesco. They have been thoroughly tested and all the ingredients are normally available at larger Tesco stores, when in season. There is no need for any special kitchen equipment.

Using the recipes

1 Both metric and imperial weights and measures are given, except for goods sold in standard size packaging, such as cans. As conversions cannot always be exact, you should follow either the metric or the imperial throughout the recipe where possible.

2 British standard level spoon measurements are used. A tablespoon measure is equivalent to 15ml; a teaspoon measure is equivalent to 5ml.

3 Dishes cooked in the oven should be placed in the centre, unless otherwise stated. Tesco advises that all meat, poultry, fish and eggs should be cooked thoroughly. Poultry juices should run clear when the flesh is pierced with a skewer at its thickest point.

4 Some of the recipes include nuts or nut derivatives. These should not be eaten by children, people who have an allergic reaction to nuts, or women who are either pregnant or breastfeeding. It is advisable to check the labelling of any commercially prepared products to ensure that they do not contain nuts or nut derivatives. Recipes that include honey should not be eaten by children under the age of 12 months.

5 Vegetables and fruits are medium-sized, unless otherwise stated. If cooking or serving vegetables or fruits with their skins on, make sure that they are thoroughly rinsed.

6 The fat and calorie content of each recipe is given. These figures are for one serving only. Any dish that has a high fat content is intended for a special occasion.

7 Each recipe has a simplicity rating of 1, 2 or 3 chef hats. Recipes with 1 hat are easy; those with 2 or 3 will require a little more effort.

CHICKEN AND LEEK SOUP WITH HERB DUMPLINGS

Serves 4

Preparation 25 mins

Cooking 1 hr 45 mins

Calories 671

Fat 37g

Simplicity

1 Place the chicken thighs, onion, carrot and herbs in a saucepan with 1.5 litres (2¾ pints) of water. Simmer, covered, for 1 hour. Strain the stock and skim off any fat. Finely chop the chicken, discarding the skin and bones. Heat half the butter in a saucepan. Add the potatoes and two-thirds of the leeks, cover and cook for 10 minutes. Pour in 1 litre (1¾ pints) of the stock and season. Simmer for 10-15 minutes, until softened. Blend until smooth in a food processor, or use a hand blender, then stir in the cooked chicken.

2 To make the dumplings, mix together the flour, breadcrumbs, suet, herbs and seasoning. Stir in 4 tablespoons of water, then shape into 8 dumplings. Cook in simmering salted water for 15-20 minutes.

3 Meanwhile, heat the rest of the butter in a frying pan. Cook the chicken breast for 4-5 minutes. Add the remaining leek and cook for 2-3 minutes, until tender, then add to the soup with the tarragon and more stock, if necessary. Bring to the boil and simmer for 2 minutes. Remove from the heat and stir in the cream. Divide between 4 serving bowls. Drain the dumplings and add 2 to each bowl.

4 chicken thighs on the bone

1 onion, chopped

1 carrot, chopped

Herb bundle made up of fresh tarragon, parsley and a bay leaf

50g (2oz) butter

300g (11oz) potatoes, cubed

3 large leeks, sliced

Salt and black pepper

2 boneless skinless chicken breasts, cut into small pieces

2 tsp chopped fresh tarragon

142ml carton single cream

For the dumplings

100g (3½oz) self-raising flour

25g (1oz) fresh white breadcrumbs

50g (2oz) shredded suet

3 tbsp chopped fresh herbs, such as tarragon, parsley or chives

With its generous portions and delicious herby dumplings, this creamy soup is almost a meal in itself.

PEA AND FRESH MINT SOUP

Simplicity 👨‍🍳

Serves 4
Preparation 15 mins
Cooking 25 mins

Calories 335
Fat 25g

50g (2oz) butter

2 rashers rindless streaky bacon, chopped

Bunch of spring onions, chopped

450g (1lb) shelled fresh peas, or frozen peas

2 Little Gem lettuces, shredded

Salt and black pepper

2 tbsp chopped fresh mint

142ml carton single cream

Pinch of caster sugar (optional)

Fresh lemon juice (optional)

Single cream to serve and snipped fresh chives to garnish

1 Melt the butter in a large heavy-based saucepan, add the bacon and cook for 2-3 minutes, then add the spring onions. Cover and cook gently for 5 minutes, stirring once or twice, until the onions have softened but not browned.

2 Add the peas and lettuce and 900ml (1½ pints) of water. Season well, bring to the boil, then simmer for 10 minutes or until the vegetables are tender. Purée with the mint and cream until smooth, using a food processor or a hand blender.

3 Return the soup to the pan. Season again, if necessary, then add the caster sugar and lemon juice, if using. Reheat gently but do not allow the soup to boil. Serve in bowls with a spoonful of cream drizzled over and a sprinkling of chives.

Fresh green peas and mint are a classic British summer combination. At other times of the year, you can use frozen peas; the soup will be sweeter but just as delicious.

PRAWN AND GRAPEFRUIT COCKTAIL

Serves 4

Preparation 20 mins

Calories 399

Fat 27g

Simplicity

1 Finely grate 1 teaspoon of grapefruit rind and reserve for the dressing. Slice the top and bottom off each grapefruit, then cut off the peel and pith, following the curve of the fruit. Cut between the membranes to release the segments and reserve.

2 To make the dressing, place the mayonnaise in a bowl, then stir in the vinegar, ketchup, Tabasco, if using, and Worcestershire sauce to taste. Stir in the grated grapefruit rind, tarragon and soured cream, then season.

3 Arrange the lettuce in serving bowls. Set aside 4 prawns for garnish, then shell the remainder. Rinse and dry on kitchen towels, then mix with the grapefruit segments and heap onto the lettuce. Spoon over the dressing, sprinkle with paprika, then garnish with the unpeeled prawns. Serve with lemon wedges.

2 pink or ruby red grapefruit

2 Little Gem lettuces, shredded

450g (1lb) large cooked shell-on prawns, defrosted if frozen

Paprika for dusting

Lemon wedges to serve

For the dressing

6 tbsp mayonnaise

1 tbsp tarragon white wine vinegar

2 tbsp tomato ketchup

Few drops Tabasco sauce (optional)

1-2 tsp Worcestershire sauce

2 tsp chopped fresh tarragon

2 tbsp soured cream

Salt and black pepper

The refreshing flavour of pink grapefruit cuts through this starter's rich and spicy dressing. Serve with thin slices of toast or some lightly buttered brown bread.

CRAB SALAD WITH TOMATO DRESSING

Simplicity

Serves 4

Preparation 15 mins

Calories 256

Fat 20g

2 large dressed crabs (about 250g (9oz) crabmeat)

1 large bulb fennel, thinly sliced, and feathery top chopped and reserved to garnish

80g bag mixed salad leaves

1 tbsp snipped fresh chives and paprika or cayenne pepper to garnish

For the dressing

2 large tomatoes

5 tbsp olive oil

1 tbsp white wine vinegar

4 tbsp single cream

1 tsp chopped fresh tarragon

Salt and black pepper

Pinch of caster sugar

Dash of Worcestershire sauce

5cm (2in) piece cucumber, diced

1 To make the dressing, place the tomatoes in a bowl and cover with boiling water. Leave for 30 seconds, then skin, deseed and cut into small dice. Whisk together the oil and vinegar in a bowl, then whisk in the cream, tarragon and seasoning. Add sugar and Worcestershire sauce to taste, then stir in the tomatoes and cucumber.

2 Mix together the crabmeat and sliced fennel and stir in 4 tablespoons of the dressing. Arrange the salad leaves together with the crab mixture on plates. Spoon over the remaining dressing, then sprinkle with the chives, chopped fennel top and paprika or cayenne pepper.

This salad combines fresh crab with fennel and a creamy dressing. If dressed crabs are unavailable, ask the fishmonger to remove the meat from whole ones for you.

POTTED CHICKEN AND HAM

Serves 4

Preparation 25 mins
plus 10 mins cooling and
3 hrs chilling

Cooking 5 mins

Calories 477

Fat 45g

Simplicity

1 To clarify the butter, place it in a small saucepan and melt over a low heat for 3-4 minutes, taking care not to let it brown. Line a sieve with damp muslin, place over a bowl and pour the butter into the sieve, discarding the milky deposit left in the pan. Leave the strained liquid (clarified butter) to cool for 5-10 minutes.

2 Meanwhile, blend the chicken or turkey and the ham until fairly smooth in a food processor. Add the pepper, nutmeg, allspice and cayenne to taste and blend until combined. Gradually pour in just under three-quarters of the clarified butter, blending all the time until mixed.

3 Spoon the mixture into small dishes or ramekins and top each with a bay leaf. Pour over the remaining butter to seal, then refrigerate for 2-3 hours, or overnight.

200g (7oz) butter

200g (7oz) cooked skinless chicken or turkey, cut into pieces

100g (3½oz) cooked ham, cut into pieces

Black pepper

¼ tsp ground nutmeg

Pinch of ground allspice

Pinch of cayenne pepper

4 fresh bay leaves

Potted meats are a great British tradition. Take off some of the richness by serving them with plenty of toast and your favourite chutney. There's no need for extra butter!

POTATO CAKES WITH SMOKED SALMON

Simplicity 👨‍🍳 👨‍🍳

Serves 4

Preparation 15 mins

Cooking 40 mins

Calories 303

Fat 18g

300g (11oz) floury potatoes such as King Edward, unpeeled

Salt and black pepper

150ml (¼ pint) full-fat milk

1 large egg

25g (1oz) plain flour

4 spring onions, finely sliced

1 tbsp oil

100ml (4fl oz) crème fraîche

2 tbsp chopped fresh dill, plus extra to garnish

150g (5oz) smoked salmon slices

Lemon wedges to serve

1 Cook the potatoes in boiling salted water for 15-20 minutes, until tender, then drain. Cool for a few minutes, then peel. Mash with the milk, season, then beat in the egg, flour and spring onions to make a batter.

2 Heat a heavy-based non-stick frying pan, then add a little of the oil. Make 4 potato cakes, using 2 tablespoons of batter for each. Fry for 2-3 minutes on each side until golden. Drain on kitchen towels and keep warm while you make 2 further batches of 4 potato cakes.

3 Mix together the crème fraîche and chopped dill. Serve the pancakes topped with the salmon slices and a spoonful of the herby crème fraîche. Grind over black pepper. Garnish with dill and the lemon wedges.

Fluffy golden potato cakes topped with smoked salmon, crème fraîche, plenty of black pepper and a squeeze of lemon juice – who could ask for anything more?

DEVILLED WHITEBAIT

Serves 4

Preparation 10 mins

Cooking 15 mins

Calories 552

Fat 50g

Simplicity

1 Heat the oil in a deep heavy-based saucepan. To check that the oil is hot enough for frying, drop in a cube of bread; it should turn brown and rise to the surface in 30 seconds.

2 Meanwhile, place the flour in a large plastic bag and add ½ teaspoon of salt, black pepper, the cayenne pepper and coriander. Shake to mix, then add the whitebait to the bag a few at a time and shake gently to coat.

3 Fry the whitebait in batches for 4-5 minutes, until crisp and golden, then drain on kitchen towels. Fry the parsley for 30-45 seconds, taking care as the fat will spit, then drain on kitchen towels. Sprinkle the whitebait with salt and serve with the deep-fried parsley and lemon wedges.

Sunflower or groundnut oil for deep-frying
5 tbsp plain flour
Salt and black pepper
¼-½ tsp cayenne pepper
1 tsp ground coriander
400g (14oz) frozen whitebait, defrosted, rinsed and dried
30g bag parsley
Lemon wedges to serve

Hot crispy whitebait served with tartare sauce has long been a British favourite. Although they're filling, you're bound to finish them, so plan to have a light main course.

ASPARAGUS WITH LEMON SAUCE

Simplicity 🍳 🍳

Serves 4

Preparation 15 mins

Cooking 20 mins

Calories 249

Fat 22g

2 bundles asparagus, about 550g (1lb 4oz) in total

Salt and black pepper

For the sauce

2 medium eggs

2 tbsp chopped pickled cucumber or gherkins

1 tsp capers, rinsed, dried and chopped

1 tsp Dijon mustard

5 tbsp olive oil

Finely grated rind and juice of ½ lemon

Pinch of caster sugar (optional)

2 tbsp finely chopped fresh parsley

2 tbsp crème fraîche or fromage frais

1 First make the sauce. Place the eggs in a pan of cold water, bring to the boil and cook for 10 minutes or until hard boiled. Peel, halve and remove the yolks, discarding the whites.

2 Mash the yolks in a bowl with the cucumber or gherkins. Stir in the capers and mustard, then gradually beat in the oil. Alternatively, blend in a food processor or with a hand blender. Beat in the lemon rind, juice and sugar, if using, then stir in the parsley and crème fraîche or fromage frais.

3 Cut the tough ends off the asparagus, then peel the lower 5cm (2in) using a vegetable peeler. Fill a saucepan with water to a depth of about 4cm (1½in), add a little salt, then bring to the boil. Stand the asparagus spears in the pan, keeping the tips out of the water. Simmer for 5-6 minutes, until just tender, then drain. Serve the asparagus with the sauce and grind over black pepper.

Sweet and tender British asparagus is among the best in the world. It's great served with this piquant lemon sauce and a generous amount of freshly ground black pepper.

STILTON AND WALNUT STUFFED MUSHROOMS

Serves 4

Preparation 20 mins

Cooking 40 mins

Calories 467

Fat 39g

Simplicity

1 Preheat the oven to 190°C/375°F/Gas Mark 5. Remove the mushroom stems and finely chop together with 3 of the mushroom caps.

2 Heat 2 tablespoons of the oil in a frying pan, then add the onion, garlic and chopped mushrooms and cook for 5-6 minutes, until soft. Transfer to a bowl, then stir in the breadcrumbs, walnuts, 1½ tablespoons each of the parsley and chives, the lemon rind and Stilton. Season well.

3 Place the 12 whole mushroom caps in a large ovenproof dish or roasting tin and divide the stuffing between them. Scatter with Parmesan, if using, and drizzle with the remaining oil. Bake for 30-35 minutes, basting once, until the mushrooms are tender and the tops have browned.

4 Stir the remaining herbs and the cucumber into the crème fraîche and serve with the stuffed mushrooms.

15 open mushrooms, about 7.5-10cm (3-4in) across

4 tbsp olive oil

1 small onion, chopped

1 clove garlic, finely chopped

100g (3½oz) fresh wholemeal breadcrumbs

50g (2oz) walnut pieces

3 tbsp chopped fresh parsley

3 tbsp snipped fresh chives

Finely grated rind of ½ lemon

125g (4oz) Stilton, crumbled

Salt and black pepper

50g (2oz) Parmesan, freshly grated (optional)

7.5cm (3in) piece cucumber, finely diced

100ml (4fl oz) crème fraîche

These creamy but crunchy stuffed mushrooms and their cooling cucumber dip make a fabulous starter. Serve them with some bread and they'll do for a main course too.

BREADED LAMB CHOPS WITH PARSNIP MASH

Simplicity 👨‍🍳 👨‍🍳

Serves 4

Preparation 15 mins

Cooking 20 mins

Calories 804

Fat 50g

2 tsp Dijon mustard

2 tsp clear honey

2 cloves garlic, crushed

1 tbsp chopped fresh rosemary, plus extra sprigs to garnish

3 tbsp olive oil or melted butter

Salt and black pepper

8 lamb loin chops

100g (3½oz) fine white fresh breadcrumbs

For the parsnip mash

450g (1lb) parsnips, cut into chunks

450g (1lb) floury potatoes, such as King Edward, cut into chunks

2 cloves garlic

50g (2oz) butter

5 tbsp single cream

Freshly grated nutmeg

1 Mix together the mustard, honey, garlic, rosemary and 2 tablespoons of the oil or butter. Season well with pepper. Thickly brush the mixture all over the chops, then coat with the breadcrumbs.

2 To make the mash, cook the parsnips, potatoes and garlic in a saucepan of boiling salted water for 15-20 minutes, until tender. Drain well, then mash with the butter and cream until smooth. Season with salt, pepper and nutmeg.

3 Meanwhile, preheat the grill to medium-high. Place the chops on the grill rack and drizzle with the remaining oil or butter. Grill for 7-8 minutes on each side, until tender – adjust the heat, if necessary, to ensure that the breadcrumbs don't burn. Serve the chops with the mash and garnish with rosemary.

The crunchy coating seals in the flavour of these rich lamb chops and goes beautifully with the sweet parsnip mash and a generous dollop of redcurrant jelly.

LANCASHIRE HOTPOT

Serves 4

Preparation 20 mins

Cooking 2 hrs 20 mins

Calories 617

Fat 35g

Simplicity

40g (1½oz) butter or dripping
4 large lamb loin chops or 8 lamb cutlets, trimmed
750g (1lb 11oz) potatoes, thinly sliced
2 large onions, sliced
3 large carrots, sliced
Salt and black pepper
400ml (14fl oz) lamb stock

1 Preheat the oven to 200°C/400°F/Gas Mark 6. Heat 25g (1oz) of the butter or dripping in a frying pan and cook the chops or cutlets for 5 minutes on each side to brown. Arrange half the potatoes in a large casserole dish, and top with half the onions, then half the carrots, seasoning each layer lightly. Add the chops or cutlets and a final layer each of onions, carrots and potatoes, again seasoning each layer. Pour over the stock, then dot with the remaining butter or dripping.

2 Cover the casserole and cook for 30 minutes. Reduce the oven temperature to 150°C/300°F/ Gas Mark 2 and cook for a further hour. Increase the oven temperature to 200°C/400°F/Gas Mark 6, then uncover the dish and cook for 30-40 minutes, until the potatoes have browned.

Layers of potato, onions and carrots sandwich tender loin chops in this traditional hotpot. It's a meal in itself – all it needs is a glass of ale or cider to wash it down.

STUFFED ROAST PORK AND SPICED APPLE SAUCE

Simplicity 🎩 🎩

Serves 6

Preparation 30 mins
plus 15 mins resting

Cooking 2 hrs 20 mins

Calories 613

Fat 39g

---

2 tbsp vegetable oil

2 onions, 1 chopped, 1 sliced

1 clove garlic, finely chopped

125g (4oz) fresh breadcrumbs

Finely grated rind of ½ lemon

1 large cooking apple, grated

1 tbsp chopped fresh sage

3 tbsp chopped fresh parsley

Salt and black pepper

1.3kg (3lb) boneless pork joint

For the sauce

1 cooking apple, chopped

1 eating apple, chopped

3 tbsp dry cider or apple juice

2.5cm (1in) piece fresh root
ginger, very finely chopped

5cm (2in) cinnamon stick

1 tsp light muscovado sugar

Squeeze of lemon juice

15g (½oz) butter

---

1 Preheat the oven to 220°C/425°F/Gas Mark 7. To make the stuffing, heat the oil in a heavy-based frying pan and cook the chopped onion and garlic for 6 minutes or until soft. Remove from the heat, and mix in the breadcrumbs, lemon rind, apple, sage and parsley, then season.

2 Open out the pork, season, then spread with the stuffing. Wrap the pork round the stuffing and tie with string. Place the sliced onion in a roasting tin, put the pork on top, then roast for 35 minutes. Reduce the oven temperature to 190°C/375°F/Gas Mark 5 and roast for 1½ hours or until the pork is cooked. Cover with foil and rest for 15 minutes.

3 To make the sauce, place the apples, cider or apple juice, ginger and cinnamon stick in a small saucepan. Cover and cook for 5-8 minutes, until the apples soften, stirring once or twice. Add the sugar and lemon juice, then season. Discard the cinnamon stick, stir in the butter and spoon into a bowl. Pour any pan juices over the pork and serve with the sauce.

An apple and sage stuffing is revealed when this succulent pork joint is carved. Serve with roast potatoes and carrots.

BAKED GAMMON WITH CAPER SAUCE

Serves 4

Preparation 15 mins
plus 30 mins cooling and
15 mins resting

Cooking 1 hr 40 mins

Calories 591

Fat 33g

Simplicity

1 Place the gammon in a large saucepan and cover with water. Bring to the boil, then simmer for 10 minutes. Drain, cover with fresh water, then add the onion, carrots and herb bundle. Simmer for 1 hour or until the vegetables are tender. Leave to cool in the cooking liquid for 30 minutes.

2 Preheat the oven to 190°C/375°F/Gas Mark 5. Transfer the gammon to a roasting tin. Strain and reserve all the cooking liquid, then add 5 tablespoons to the tin. Combine the mustard and marmalade, then spread over the joint. Bake for 30 minutes, basting twice. Rest for 15 minutes before carving.

3 Meanwhile, make the sauce. Heat the butter in a saucepan, then fry the shallots for 5 minutes. Stir in the flour and cook for 2 minutes, stirring. Stir in 300ml (½ pint) of the reserved liquid and simmer for 2 minutes. Stir in the milk and cook for 20 minutes, stirring often. Add the capers, parsley, mustard and cream. Heat through, season and serve with the meat.

750g (1lb 11oz) piece boneless smoked or unsmoked gammon

1 onion, halved

2 carrots, sliced

Herb bundle made up of thyme, parsley sprigs and a bay leaf

1 tsp English mustard powder

2 tbsp orange marmalade

For the sauce

40g (1½oz) butter

2 shallots, chopped

3 tbsp plain flour

200ml (7fl oz) full-fat milk

1 tbsp capers, rinsed, dried and chopped

2 tbsp chopped fresh parsley

1 tsp Dijon mustard

2 tbsp double cream

Salt and black pepper

Sticky marmalade-glazed gammon and this mustard and caper sauce go together superbly. Serve with new potatoes.

STEAK PIE WITH GUINNESS

Simplicity 👨‍🍳 👨‍🍳

Serves 6
Preparation 30 mins
Cooking 3 hrs

Calories 628
Fat 32g

3 tbsp plain flour

1 tsp English mustard powder

Salt and black pepper

750g (1lb 11oz) stewing beef, trimmed and cut into cubes

4 tbsp vegetable oil

2 onions, sliced

2 cloves garlic, finely chopped

500ml bottle Guinness

2 tbsp Worcestershire sauce

2 bay leaves

1 tbsp chopped fresh thyme

1 tsp soft dark brown sugar

250g (9oz) chestnut mushrooms, halved if large

For the pastry crust

250g (9oz) self-raising flour

2 tsp chopped fresh thyme

125g (4oz) shredded suet

1 Preheat the oven to 180°C/350°F/Gas Mark 4. Combine the flour, mustard and pepper, then coat the beef in the mixture. Heat 2 tablespoons of oil in a heavy-based frying pan. Fry a third of the beef for 3-4 minutes, until browned. Transfer to an ovenproof dish and fry the rest of the beef in 2 more batches.

2 Add another tablespoon of oil to the pan, then fry the onions for 5 minutes. Add the garlic and cook for 2 minutes. Stir in the Guinness, Worcestershire sauce, herbs and sugar and simmer for 2-3 minutes. Pour over the beef, then cover and cook in the oven for 2 hours. Remove the beef and increase the oven temperature to 190°C/375°F/ Gas Mark 5. Fry the mushrooms in the rest of the oil. Stir into the beef, then transfer to a 15 x 20cm (6 x 8in) pie dish.

3 Sift together the flour and ½ teaspoon of salt, then add the thyme and pepper. Stir in the suet and bind with 10-12 tablespoons of water to form a soft dough. Roll it out, dampen the edges of the dish and cover with the pastry. Trim, then make a small slit in the centre. Cook for 30-40 minutes, until golden.

Guinness adds its creamy richness to this slow-cooked steak pie. Serve it with mash and peas or cabbage.

CLAPSHOT PIE

Serves 6

Preparation 20 mins

Cooking 1 hr 55 mins

Calories 397

Fat 21g

Simplicity

1 Heat the oil in a frying pan, then fry the onion, carrot and bacon for 10 minutes or until browned. Add the mince and fry for 10-15 minutes, breaking up any lumps with the back of a wooden spoon, until the meat has browned. Spoon off any excess fat, then stir in the stock, ketchup, Worcestershire sauce, thyme and seasoning. Simmer, partly covered, for 45 minutes, stirring occasionally, until thickened. Add a little water if the mixture becomes too dry.

2 Meanwhile, cook the potatoes and swede in boiling salted water for 15-20 minutes, until tender. Drain, then mash with 25g (1oz) butter and the cream. Season with pepper and nutmeg.

3 Preheat the oven to 200°C/400°F/Gas Mark 6. Transfer the beef to a 1.5 litre (2¾ pint) shallow ovenproof dish, then stir in the parsley. Smooth over the potato and swede mixture, then fluff up with a fork and dot with the remaining butter. Bake for 35-45 minutes, until browned. Garnish with parsley.

1 tbsp olive or sunflower oil

1 large onion, chopped

1 large carrot, finely chopped

50g (2oz) bacon, chopped

750g (1lb 11oz) beef steak mince

300ml (½ pint) beef stock

2 tbsp tomato ketchup

1 tbsp Worcestershire sauce

1 tsp chopped fresh thyme

Salt and black pepper

2 tbsp chopped fresh parsley, plus extra to garnish

For the topping

450g (1lb) potatoes, chopped

450g (1lb) swede, chopped

50g (2oz) butter

142ml carton single cream

Freshly grated nutmeg

Clapshot is the Scottish name for a mixture of mashed potato and swede, hence the name of this version of cottage pie.

DUCK WITH BRAISED TURNIPS

Simplicity

Serves 4
Preparation 15 mins
Cooking 50 mins

Calories 450
Fat 36g

4 duck leg joints

500g (1lb 2oz) white turnips, peeled and cut into 5cm (2in) chunks

Salt and black pepper

100ml (4fl oz) chicken stock

1 tsp caster sugar

1 tbsp fresh orange juice

1 Preheat the oven to 190°C/375°F/Gas Mark 5. Heat a non-stick frying pan, add the duck, skin-side down, then cook over a medium-high heat for 7-8 minutes, until browned. Pour off the fat that runs out and reserve. Place the duck, skin-side up, on a baking sheet and cook for 30-40 minutes, until the skin is crisp and the meat cooked through.

2 Meanwhile, cook the turnips in boiling salted water for 5-6 minutes, until softened, then drain. Place 2 tablespoons of the reserved duck fat in a large frying pan, add the turnips and fry for 5 minutes or until lightly browned. Add the stock and season.

3 Partly cover the pan and cook for 10 minutes or until the turnips are tender and almost all the liquid has evaporated. Uncover the pan, add the sugar and orange juice, then cook over a high heat for 3-4 minutes, stirring, until the turnips caramelise. Serve with the duck.

Duck and caramelised turnips are a terrific combination, especially served with savoy cabbage. You can use duck breasts too, but they'll only need 20 minutes in the oven.

ROAST PARTRIDGE WITH BACON AND SAGE

Serves 4

Preparation 15 mins

Cooking 45 mins

Calories 590

Fat 36g

Simplicity

1 Preheat the oven to 220°C/425°F/Gas Mark 7. Place a lemon quarter and 2 sage leaves or a sprinkling of dried sage in each bird. Season well, then wrap in 2 slices of bacon, tucking in 2 more sage leaves or a little more dried sage. Place in a roasting tin and drizzle with the oil. Roast, uncovered, for 30-35 minutes, basting once or twice, until tender and cooked. Remove the birds and keep warm.

2 Pour the cooking juices into a saucepan and add the stock and wine. Boil rapidly, stirring all the time, for 7 minutes or until reduced by half. Add 1 teaspoon of redcurrant jelly and boil again for 1-2 minutes. Stir in the rest of the redcurrant jelly, the vinegar and seasoning to taste.

3 Remove the pan from the heat and stir in the butter, until melted. Serve the sauce with the partridges, garnished with sage leaves, if using.

1 lemon, quartered
16 fresh sage leaves, plus extra to garnish, or 2 tsp dried sage
4 oven-ready partridges
Salt and black pepper
8 rashers thinly sliced dry-cured bacon
2 tbsp olive oil
200ml (7fl oz) chicken stock
4 tbsp red or white wine
2 tsp redcurrant jelly
1-2 tsp balsamic vinegar
15g (½oz) chilled butter, cubed

Bacon and sage-flavoured partridge with its rich wine gravy makes a spectacular change from a traditional roast. Serve with golden chunks of roasted potato.

VENISON STEAKS WITH PARSNIPS AND HORSERADISH

Simplicity

Serves 4

Preparation 20 mins

plus 4 hrs marinating

Cooking 15 mins

Calories 509

Fat 27g

7 tbsp olive oil

1 tbsp balsamic vinegar

4 tbsp port

1 tsp juniper berries, crushed

1 onion, sliced

2 x 340g packs venison steaks

Salt and black pepper

150ml (¼ pint) chicken or beef stock

1 tsp redcurrant jelly

4 large parsnips, cut into wedges

For the horseradish cream

1 tsp traditional hot horseradish

1 tsp chopped fresh tarragon

5 tbsp crème fraîche

1 Mix 2 tablespoons of the oil with the vinegar, port and juniper berries. Put the onion and venison into a shallow non-metallic dish, season, then pour over the marinade. Cover and refrigerate for 4 hours or overnight, turning once. Drain the venison on kitchen towels. Reserve the marinade.

2 Heat 1 tablespoon of oil in a large heavy-based frying pan, then fry the steaks for 4-5 minutes, until browned. Turn over and cook for 3-4 minutes more. Remove and keep warm. Strain the marinade and add with the stock to the pan, then boil for 3-4 minutes, until reduced by half. Stir in the redcurrant jelly and cook for 2 minutes. Season.

3 Meanwhile, preheat the grill to medium. Place the parsnips on a baking tray and brush with 2 tablespoons of the oil. Season and grill for 5-6 minutes, then turn, brush with the remaining oil and cook for a further 5 minutes or until golden. To make the horseradish cream, mix together the horseradish, tarragon and crème fraîche. Serve with the venison, parsnips and redcurrant sauce.

Port and juniper berries flavour a marinade, which slowly tenderises the venison steaks. The end result is fabulous.

DOVER SOLE WITH CREAMED CUCUMBER SAUCE

Serves 4

Preparation 15 mins

plus 1 hr standing

Cooking 50 mins

Calories 615

Fat 41g

Simplicity

1 Place the cucumber in a colander and sprinkle with salt, tossing to mix. Leave to stand for 1 hour, then rinse and dry. Melt the unsalted butter in a saucepan over a low heat and bubble for 3-4 minutes without browning. Line a sieve with damp muslin, place over a bowl and carefully pour in the butter, discarding the milky deposit left in the pan. Leave the strained liquid (clarified butter) to cool.

2 Meanwhile, heat the butter for the sauce in a saucepan, add the shallots and cook for 5 minutes to soften. Add the cucumber and fry for 10 minutes, stirring occasionally. Stir in the vinegar and wine, and cook briskly for 5-8 minutes, until only 1-2 tablespoons of liquid remain in the pan. Add the cream and tarragon and heat for 1-2 minutes. Season.

3 Season the flour with salt and pepper, then coat the fish in the mixture. Heat the clarified butter in a frying pan, then fry half the fish for 3-5 minutes on each side, until golden. Drain on kitchen towels, then keep warm while you cook the remaining fish. Serve with the cucumber sauce and lemon slices.

125g (4oz) unsalted butter
5 tbsp plain flour
Salt and black pepper
8 Dover sole fillets
Lemon slices to serve

For the sauce

1 cucumber, peeled, halved lengthways, deseeded and sliced
1 tsp salt
25g (1oz) butter
2 shallots, finely chopped
4 tbsp tarragon white wine vinegar
4 tbsp dry white wine
4 tbsp double cream
2 tsp chopped fresh tarragon

Dover sole is best served very simply. This creamy sauce is delicate enough not to overpower the flavour of the fish.

SALMON WITH CHAMP AND TOMATO SALAD

Simplicity

Serves 4

Preparation 20 mins

Cooking 30 mins

Calories 702

Fat 42g

50g (2oz) fresh white breadcrumbs

6 tbsp chopped fresh basil, plus extra leaves to garnish

2 tbsp snipped fresh chives

4 tbsp olive oil

Finely grated rind and juice of ½ lime

4 salmon fillets, about 175g (6oz) each

200g (7oz) cherry tomatoes, halved

For the champ

750g (1lb 11oz) potatoes, cut into even-sized chunks

Salt and black pepper

200ml (7fl oz) half-fat milk

40g (1½oz) butter

Bunch of spring onions, chopped

1 First make the champ. Cook the potatoes in boiling salted water for 15 minutes or until tender. Place the milk, butter and all but 2 tablespoons of the chopped spring onions in a saucepan and heat to just below boiling point. Drain and mash the potatoes, then stir in the milk mixture and season. Keep warm.

2 Meanwhile, preheat the oven to 200°C/400°F/ Gas Mark 6. Mix the breadcrumbs with half the basil and half the chives. Add 3 tablespoons of oil, the lime rind and seasoning. Place the salmon on a baking sheet and press the breadcrumb mixture onto the top and sides. Bake for 15 minutes or until the top is golden and the salmon is cooked.

3 While the salmon is cooking, whisk the remaining tablespoon of oil with 1 tablespoon of lime juice in a bowl, then add the tomatoes, the reserved spring onions and the remaining basil and chives. Season to taste. Serve the tomato salad with the salmon and champ, garnished with basil.

Champ, or Irish mash, goes particularly well with this herb-crusted salmon and a light cherry tomato salad.

FISH CAKES WITH TARTARE SAUCE

Serves 4

Preparation 35 mins

plus 1 hr chilling

Cooking 50 mins

Calories 726

Fat 43g

Simplicity

1 Cook the potatoes in boiling salted water for 15 minutes or until tender. Drain, then mash and leave to cool. Meanwhile, place the fish in a frying pan and pour over the milk. Cook over a low heat, partly covered, for 10 minutes or until just cooked. Remove from the milk and flake, discarding any skin or bones.

2 Mix together the fish, mash, parsley and spring onions and season well. Shape into 8 cakes, 2cm (¾in) thick. Season the flour with salt and pepper. Dip the fish cakes into the seasoned flour, then the beaten egg, and finally the breadcrumbs, coating well. Refrigerate for 1 hour.

3 To make the tartare sauce, mix the mayonnaise with the crème fraîche, capers, gherkins, herbs, lemon rind and pepper.

4 Heat 5mm (¼in) oil in a frying pan and fry half the fish cakes for 5-6 minutes on each side, until golden. Drain on kitchen towels, then keep warm while you cook the rest. Serve with the tartare sauce.

450g (1lb) potatoes, cut into chunks

Salt and black pepper

500g (1lb 2oz) cod fillets

200ml (7fl oz) full-fat milk

2 tbsp chopped fresh parsley

4 spring onions, finely sliced

4 tbsp plain flour

2 medium eggs, beaten

75g (3oz) dried breadcrumbs

Oil for shallow frying

For the tartare sauce

6 tbsp mayonnaise

2 tbsp crème fraîche

1 tbsp capers, rinsed, dried and chopped

2 tbsp finely chopped gherkins

1 tbsp chopped fresh parsley

1 tbsp chopped fresh tarragon

½ tsp finely grated lemon rind

There's something comforting about eating good fish cakes. These are great with lightly cooked cabbage and carrots.

SMOKED HADDOCK STEW WITH LEEK AND BACON

Simplicity 🍳 🍳

Serves 4

Preparation 20 mins
plus 10 mins standing

Cooking 35 mins

Calories 572

Fat 33g

750ml (1¼ pints) full-fat milk

2 bay leaves

3 leeks, 1 cut in half lengthways, 2 thickly sliced

500g (1lb 2oz) smoked haddock fillet

25g (1oz) butter

125g (4oz) rindless dry-cured smoked streaky bacon, cut into 4cm (1½in) wide strips

500g (1lb 2oz) potatoes, cut into 3cm (1¼in) chunks

Salt and black pepper

142ml carton single cream

Lemon juice (optional)

2 tbsp chopped fresh parsley

2 tbsp snipped fresh chives to garnish

1 Place the milk, bay leaves, halved leek and haddock in a saucepan. Bring to the boil, then simmer for 2-3 minutes. Cover the pan and set aside for 10 minutes. Remove the haddock, discard any skin and bones, flake the flesh and set aside. Discard the leek but reserve the milk and bay leaves.

2 Heat the butter in a large heavy-based frying pan and fry the bacon for 2-3 minutes, until its fat starts to melt. Add the sliced leeks and cook for 5 minutes or until softened. Add the potatoes and cook for 3-4 minutes, until softened slightly.

3 Add the reserved milk, bay leaves and 150ml (¼ pint) of water. Season, bring to the boil, then cover and simmer for 15 minutes. Discard the bay leaves. Blend half the mixture with half the haddock using a hand blender, or mash with a potato masher; return to the pan. Stir in the remaining haddock and cream; reheat gently. Season and add lemon juice to taste, if using. Stir in the parsley. Sprinkle with chives.

This stew is based on the Scottish soup, cullen skink, and has a wonderfully rich smoky flavour. Served with chunks of warm soda bread, it's a really satisfying meal.

MIXED SHELLFISH AND POTATO SALAD

Serves 4

Preparation 25 mins

plus 30 mins cooling

Cooking 30 mins

Calories 396

Fat 16g

Simplicity

1 To make the dressing, whisk together the oil, vinegar, mustard and seasoning. Boil the potatoes in salted water for 15 minutes or until tender, then drain. Cool for 30 minutes, then peel and slice. Place in a bowl and toss with half the dressing. Toss the beetroot and fennel with the rest of the dressing.

2 Scrub the mussels and cockles under cold running water, pulling away any beards from the mussels. Discard any shellfish that are open or damaged. Place the wine or cider and shallot in a large saucepan and bring to the boil. Simmer for 2 minutes, then add the shellfish. Cover and cook briskly for 3-5 minutes, shaking the pan often, or until opened. Discard any that remain closed. Reserve the pan juices, set aside a few mussels in their shells and shell the rest.

3 Boil the pan juices for 5 minutes or until reduced to 1-2 tablespoons. Strain over the potatoes. Add the shellfish, spring onions and parsley, then toss. Serve with the beetroot and fennel salad and garnish with the fennel tops and mussels in their shells.

750g (1lb 11oz) waxy potatoes, such as Charlotte, unpeeled

4 small cooked beetroot, diced

1 head fennel, finely sliced, plus feathery top, chopped

1kg (2lb 4oz) mussels

500g (1lb 2oz) cockles

300ml (½ pint) dry white wine or dry cider

1 shallot, finely chopped

4 spring onions, finely sliced

3 tbsp chopped fresh parsley

For the dressing

5 tbsp olive oil

1½ tbsp cider vinegar

½ tsp English mustard

Salt and black pepper

This dish is really two salads in one. It uses great British foods – cockles, mussels, potatoes, fennel and beetroot.

GLAMORGAN SAUSAGES WITH TOMATO SALAD

Simplicity

Serves 4

Preparation 20 mins

plus 15 mins cooling and

1 hr chilling

Cooking 35 mins

Calories 540

Fat 35g

100g (3½oz) potato

Salt and black pepper

100g (3½oz) white breadcrumbs

150g (5oz) Lancashire or
Caerphilly cheese, grated

1 small leek, finely chopped

¼ tsp dried sage

1 tbsp chopped fresh parsley

Pinch of cayenne pepper

1 medium egg, plus 2 egg yolks

3 tbsp plain flour

Oil for shallow frying

For the salad

3 tbsp olive oil

2 tsp balsamic vinegar

Pinch of brown sugar

150g (5oz) cherry tomatoes

1 red onion, thinly sliced

5cm (2in) piece cucumber, sliced

Few fresh basil leaves

---

1 Cook the potato in boiling salted water for 15-20 minutes, until tender. Drain well, mash, then leave to cool for 15 minutes. Mix the cold mash with half the breadcrumbs, the cheese, leek, sage and parsley. Season with salt, pepper and cayenne. Bind together with the yolks. Using your hands, shape into 12 sausages. Cover and refrigerate for 1 hour.

2 Season the flour. Beat the whole egg. Dip the sausages into the seasoned flour, then into the beaten egg, then coat in the remaining breadcrumbs. Heat 5mm (¼in) of oil in a large frying pan and fry half the sausages, turning, for 10 minutes or until golden brown. Drain on kitchen towels and keep warm while you cook the rest.

3 Meanwhile, make the salad. Whisk together the oil, vinegar and sugar. Halve the tomatoes and toss in the dressing with the onion, cucumber and basil. Season and serve with the sausages.

Glamorgan sausages are usually made with Caerphilly, but a good Lancashire produces equally delicious results.

MIXED VEGETABLE CHEESE BAKE

Serves 4

Preparation 30 mins

Cooking 1 hr 20 mins

Calories 477

Fat 31g

Simplicity

1 Preheat the oven to 200°C/400°F/Gas Mark 6. Put the squash into an ovenproof dish, season, then drizzle over half the oil. Roast for 25 minutes, stirring once, until tender. Meanwhile, cook the cauliflower in boiling salted water for 5 minutes or until just tender. Drain, reserving 200ml (7fl oz) of the cooking water, then refresh in cold water and set aside. Fry the mushrooms in the remaining oil for 4-5 minutes.

2 To make the sauce, melt the butter in a saucepan and stir in the flour and cayenne pepper. Cook for 2 minutes, then gradually stir in the reserved cooking liquid. Cook for 2-3 minutes, until thick, then gradually stir in the milk. Simmer, stirring, for 10 minutes. Remove from the heat, then stir in the mustard and the cheese, until melted. Season to taste.

3 Reduce the oven temperature to 180°C/350°F/ Gas Mark 4. Add the cauliflower to the squash, then divide between four individual ovenproof dishes. Scatter over the mushrooms and pour over the sauce. Mix the breadcrumbs and Parmesan, then sprinkle over each dish. Bake for 30-35 minutes.

1 large butternut squash, peeled, deseeded and cut into chunks

Salt and black pepper

3 tbsp olive oil

1 large cauliflower, cut into florets

350g (12oz) mushrooms, sliced

2 tbsp fresh white breadcrumbs

2 tbsp freshly grated Parmesan

For the sauce

25g (1oz) butter, plus extra for greasing

25g (1oz) plain flour

Pinch of cayenne pepper

300ml (½ pint) full-fat milk

1 tsp English mustard

100g (3½oz) Cheddar, grated

This dish is based on cauliflower cheese, but adding extra vegetables turns it into something much more exciting.

LEEK AND MUSHROOM PASTIES

Simplicity

Serves 4

Preparation 25 mins

plus 30 mins cooling

Cooking 40 mins

Calories 703

Fat 49g

40g (1½oz) butter

2 carrots, cut into matchsticks

1 tsp paprika

4 leeks, thinly sliced

2 cloves garlic, thinly sliced

250g (9oz) brown cap mushrooms, sliced

5 tbsp double cream

1-2 tsp light soy sauce

2 tbsp chopped fresh parsley

Lemon juice to taste

Salt and black pepper

500g pack puff pastry, defrosted if frozen

1 small egg, beaten

1 Preheat the oven to 200°C/400°F/Gas Mark 6. Melt the butter in a frying pan, add the carrots and paprika and fry gently for 5 minutes or until softened. Stir in the leeks and garlic and fry for 2 minutes, then add the mushrooms and fry for 5 minutes, stirring frequently, until the vegetables are tender and any liquid has evaporated.

2 Stir in the cream and soy sauce, then simmer for 2 minutes. Add the parsley and lemon juice and season. Cool for 30 minutes or until completely cold.

3 Roll out the pastry on a lightly floured surface. Cut out 4 x 20cm (8in) circles, using a saucer or small plate as a guide. Divide the filling between the circles, then fold the pastry over to form 4 pasties. Seal the pasty edges with a little beaten egg. Pinch with your fingers, then brush the tops with egg. Cook at the top of the oven for 25 minutes or until browned.

The rich flaky pastry and creamy centres make these vegetable pasties really filling. Serve with a light sauce of cucumber, mint and crème fraîche.

GOOSEBERRIES WITH ELDERFLOWER SYLLABUB

Serves 4

Preparation 20 mins

plus 8 hrs chilling and

20 mins cooling

Cooking 15 mins

Calories 408

Fat 25g

Simplicity

1 Place the lemon rind and juice, wine, nutmeg and ginger for the syllabub in a bowl. Cover and place in the fridge for 8 hours, or overnight.

2 Place the sugar, lemon strips and 150ml (¼ pint) of water in a heavy-based saucepan and bring to the boil, stirring to dissolve the sugar. Add the gooseberries and bring back to the boil. Reduce the heat and simmer for 5-8 minutes, until they are tender. Transfer the gooseberries to a bowl. Boil the syrup for 3 minutes or until thick and sticky. Leave to cool for 1-2 minutes, then strain over the gooseberries. Leave to cool for 20 minutes.

3 Strain the syllabub mixture into a large bowl, add the cream and whisk. Gradually whisk in the cordial, then continue whisking until the mixture is thick but not too stiff. Add caster sugar to taste. Spoon the gooseberry mixture into glasses, then top with the syllabub.

125g (4oz) caster sugar

2-3 strips lemon rind, pared with a vegetable peeler

300g (11oz) gooseberries, topped and tailed

For the syllabub

Finely grated rind and juice of 1 lemon

3 tbsp sweet muscat wine

½ tsp freshly grated nutmeg

¼ tsp ground ginger

200ml (7fl oz) double cream

4 tbsp elderflower cordial

Caster sugar to taste

This creamy syllabub has a lovely scent of elderflowers. Serve with thin almond biscuits for a crisp contrast.

CRANACHAN WITH RASPBERRIES

Simplicity

Serves 4

Calories 495

Preparation 15 mins

Fat 26g

Cooking 15 mins

25g (1oz) butter

40g (1½oz) soft dark brown sugar

125g (4oz) porridge oats

200g (7oz) fromage frais

142ml carton whipping cream

1-2 tbsp clear honey, plus extra for trickling (optional)

1-2 tbsp whisky

225g (8oz) raspberries

2 tbsp icing sugar

1 Preheat the oven to 160°C/325°F/Gas Mark 3. Melt the butter and sugar in a small saucepan over a low heat, then stir in the oats until well mixed. Turn onto a baking sheet and spread out. Bake for 15 minutes, stirring halfway through, until lightly toasted. Transfer to a plate and leave to cool while you prepare the cream mixture.

2 Beat the fromage frais until smooth. Whisk the cream until it forms soft peaks, then fold into the fromage frais with 1-2 tablespoons of honey and whisky to taste. Toss the fruit in the icing sugar.

3 Spoon the fromage frais mixture into bowls, top with the oats and finish with the raspberries. Trickle over the extra honey, if using.

This is one of Scotland's best! Cream is flavoured with honey and a dash of whisky, then topped with sweet toasted oats and fresh raspberries tossed in icing sugar.

RHUBARB AND STRAWBERRY CRUMBLE

Serves 4

Preparation 15 mins

Cooking 45 mins

Calories 583

Fat 34g

Simplicity

1 Preheat the oven to 180°C/350°F/Gas Mark 4. Mix together the rhubarb, strawberries and sugar. Transfer to a 20 x 30cm (8 x 12in) ovenproof dish.

2 To make the topping, sift the flour and salt into a bowl, then stir in the caster or brown sugar. Rub the butter into the mixture using your fingertips until it resembles fine breadcrumbs. Stir in the ground and slivered almonds, then sprinkle the mixture over the fruit.

3 Bake for 40-45 minutes, until the fruit juices are bubbling and the topping is lightly browned.

500g (1lb 2oz) rhubarb, cut into chunks

250g (9oz) strawberries, hulled and halved

50g (2oz) soft light brown sugar

For the topping

150g (5oz) plain flour

Pinch of salt

50g (2oz) caster or soft light brown sugar

75g (3oz) unsalted butter, cubed

75g (3oz) ground almonds

50g (2oz) slivered or flaked almonds

Almonds give this crumble its extra richness. It can be eaten hot or cold, with some lightly whipped cream, thick Greek yogurt or plenty of homemade custard.

CARAMELISED RICE PUDDING WITH APRICOTS

Simplicity

Serves 4

Preparation 15 mins
plus 25 mins cooling
and 1 hr chilling

Cooking 1 hr 30 mins

Calories 674

Fat 29g

75g (3oz) pudding rice

200g (7oz) caster sugar

2 vanilla pods, 1 split in half lengthways

25g (1oz) unsalted butter

600ml (1 pint) full-fat milk

142ml carton double cream

2 strips lemon rind and juice of 1 lemon

250g (9oz) ready-to-eat dried apricots

1-2 tbsp orange liqueur, such as Cointreau

1 Put the rice into a saucepan, cover with water and boil for 5 minutes. Drain. Return the rice to the pan with 40g (1½oz) of the sugar, the split vanilla pod, butter and milk. Simmer for 45-60 minutes, stirring often, until thickened. Transfer to a bowl and cool for 20 minutes. Remove the vanilla pod and scrape the seeds into the rice. Discard the pod. Whisk the cream until it forms soft peaks, then fold into the rice.

2 Meanwhile, put 100g (3½oz) of the sugar into a saucepan with the lemon strips, remaining vanilla pod and 200ml (7fl oz) of water. Heat, stirring, for 3 minutes or until the sugar dissolves. Add the apricots and cook for 20 minutes to reduce the syrup.

3 Put the apricots into 4 ramekins, add the lemon juice, liqueur and syrup, then cool for 5 minutes. Top with the rice pudding, then refrigerate for 1 hour. Preheat the grill to high. Sprinkle the puddings with the rest of the sugar. Grill for 1-2 minutes, until the sugar caramelises, then cool for a few minutes.

You'll forget any schoolday horrors of stodgy rice pudding

when you taste this apricot version topped with caramel.

GINGER AND PEAR STEAMED PUDDING

Serves 4

Preparation 25 mins
plus 5 mins cooling

Cooking 1 hr 30 mins

Calories 748

Fat 36g

Simplicity 🎩 🎩

1 Grease a 1.2 litre (2 pint) pudding basin with butter and coat with 1 tablespoon of sugar. Carefully line the base and sides of the basin with the pear slices, then drizzle over half the ginger syrup.

2 Beat together the butter and sugar until light and fluffy, then gradually beat in the eggs. Sift together the flour and ground ginger, then fold into the butter mixture. Stir in the breadcrumbs, lemon rind, remaining syrup, the stem ginger and the chopped pear. Spoon into the basin and level the top, then cover the basin with a double layer each of baking paper and foil. Tie a piece of string around the rim of the basin to hold the layers in place, then cut off any excess paper and foil.

3 Place the basin in a saucepan and pour in boiling water to reach halfway up the basin. Bring back to the boil, then simmer, covered, for 1½ hours, adding more water as necessary. Remove the basin from the water and leave to cool for 5 minutes. Invert onto a plate, tap the base and remove the basin.

150g (5oz) butter, softened, plus extra for greasing

150g (5oz) light muscovado sugar, plus 1 tbsp to coat

3 ripe pears, peeled and cored, 1 chopped, 2 sliced

3 pieces preserved stem ginger, chopped, and 5 tbsp syrup from the jar

2 large eggs, beaten

175g (6oz) self-raising flour

2 tsp ground ginger

25g (1oz) fresh white breadcrumbs

Finely grated rind of 1 lemon

The flavours of the ginger and pears mingle beautifully in this surprisingly light pudding. Serve with lots of custard.

TREACLE TART

Simplicity

Serves 6

Preparation 15 mins

Cooking 40 mins

Calories 487

Fat 12g

250g (9oz) shortcrust pastry, defrosted if frozen

454g can golden syrup

100g (3½oz) fresh white breadcrumbs

1 tsp ground ginger

Finely grated rind of 1 lemon and juice of ½ lemon

2 eating apples, such as Cox's, peeled, cored and coarsely grated

1 Preheat the oven to 190°C/375°F/Gas Mark 5. Roll out the pastry on a lightly floured surface and use to line a 20cm (8in) flan tin at least 2.5cm (1in) deep. Trim off the excess pastry and reserve for decoration. Line with baking paper and baking beans, then bake blind for 10-12 minutes, until the pastry is lightly golden. Remove the paper and beans.

2 Meanwhile, make the filling. Open the can of syrup and place in a saucepan. Pour in boiling water to reach halfway up the tin. Warm over a low heat for 5 minutes or until the syrup is very runny. Place the breadcrumbs, ginger, lemon rind and juice and apples in a bowl. Pour over the syrup and mix.

3 Pour the mixture into the pastry case. Roll out the reserved pastry and cut into strips, then twist gently. Lay the strips in a criss-cross pattern on top of the tart. Bake for 25-30 minutes, until bubbling.

Treacle tart has been a British favourite for centuries. Golden syrup is used rather than treacle these days, but the pudding has kept its name. Serve with vanilla ice cream.

APPLE DUMPLINGS WITH BUTTERSCOTCH SAUCE

Serves 6

Preparation 30 mins

plus 1 hr chilling

Cooking 50 mins

Calories 770

Fat 50g

Simplicity

1 To make the sauce, place the butter, sugar and cream in a heavy-based saucepan and stir until the butter melts. Boil for 2-3 minutes, until thickened, then add lemon juice to taste. Set aside.

2 Roll out the pastry on a lightly floured surface and cut out 6 circles just large enough to enclose the apples. Cut some leaves from the trimmings for decoration. Place the circles on a baking sheet.

3 Combine the pecans, dates and cinnamon with 6 tablespoons of the sauce. Cut out the centre of each apple to remove the core. Put an apple on each pastry circle, then half-fill with the pecan mixture. Gather up the pastry, brush the edges with egg mixture and pinch together, then brush all over with the egg mixture and decorate with the reserved pastry leaves. Refrigerate for 1 hour.

4 Preheat the oven to 190°C/375°F/Gas Mark 5. Bake for 35-45 minutes, until the pastry is golden and the apples are tender. Gently reheat the remaining sauce and serve with the apples.

500g pack fresh puff or shortcrust pastry

25g (1oz) shelled pecans, chopped

25g (1oz) stoned dates, finely chopped

½ tsp ground cinnamon

6 eating apples, such as Cox's, peeled

1 small egg yolk, beaten with 2 tbsp milk

For the sauce

75g (3oz) butter

150g (5oz) light muscovado sugar

142ml carton double cream

Lemon juice to taste

Hidden inside these pastry-covered apples is a wonderful mixture of crunchy pecan nuts and cinnamon-spiced dates.

BAKEWELL TART WITH PLUMS

Simplicity 🍳 🍳

Serves 6

Preparation 20 mins
plus 30 mins chilling

Cooking 1 hr 15 mins

Calories 751

Fat 49g

175g (6oz) plain flour

40g (1½oz) icing sugar

75g (3oz) butter, diced

1 medium egg yolk

Juice of ½ lemon

For the filling

450g (1lb) plums, halved, stoned and chopped

175g (6oz) caster sugar

125g (4oz) unsalted butter, softened

2 medium eggs, beaten

150g (5oz) ground almonds

Few drops almond extract (optional)

50g (2oz) flaked almonds

---

1 Sift the flour and icing sugar into a bowl, add the butter and rub in using your fingertips until the mixture resembles fine breadcrumbs. Add the egg yolk and lemon juice and mix to a dough. Cover and refrigerate for 30 minutes.

2 Preheat the oven to 190°C/375°F/Gas Mark 5. Use the pastry to line a deep 20cm (8in) metal flan tin. Line with baking paper and baking beans, then bake blind for 10-12 minutes, until the pastry is golden. Set aside, then reduce the oven temperature to 180°C/350°F/Gas Mark 4.

3 Cook the plums with 50g (2oz) of sugar in a saucepan for 10 minutes or until soft. Cool, drain, discarding the syrup, then spread over the pastry case. Beat the butter and remaining sugar together, until light and fluffy. Beat in the eggs a little at a time, then beat in the ground almonds and extract if using. Smooth the filling over the plums, sprinkle with the flaked almonds, then bake for 50 minutes or until the filling is set.

This tart was originally known as Bakewell pudding and it proves that old-fashioned things are sometimes the best.

WENSLEYDALE AND APPLE SCONES

Makes 10-12 scones

Preparation 20 mins

Cooking 15 mins

Calories 195 each

Fat 10g each

Simplicity

1 Preheat the oven to 200°C/400°F/Gas Mark 6. Grease a baking sheet.

2 Sift the flour, baking powder and a good pinch of salt into a bowl, then stir in the oatmeal, mustard powder and sugar. Rub in the butter using your fingertips until it resembles fine breadcrumbs. Stir in the cheese and apples and bind with just enough soured cream or buttermilk to make a soft but not sticky dough.

3 Roll out the dough on a floured surface to about 2cm (¾in) thick and stamp out 8 scones, using a 6cm (2½in) pastry cutter. Without overhandling the dough, press the trimmings together and roll out again to make more scones. Place on the baking sheet, brush the tops with soured cream or buttermilk and lightly dust with oatmeal. Bake for 15 minutes, then cool on a wire rack for a few minutes before serving.

50g (2oz) butter, cubed, plus extra for greasing

200g (7oz) self-raising flour

1 tsp baking powder

Salt

50g (2oz) fine oatmeal, plus extra for dusting

½ tsp English mustard powder

1 tsp light muscovado sugar

125g (4oz) Wensleydale cheese, cut into 1cm (½in) cubes

1 large or 2 small eating apples, peeled, cored and chopped into 5mm (¼in) pieces

4-5 tablespoons soured cream or buttermilk, plus extra for glazing

In Yorkshire, the local Wensleydale cheese is often served with apple pie. These scones bring together the same blend of sweet and savoury. Try them with clotted cream.

INDEX

The Tesco Cookery Series

Fast Family Meals • Great Value Meals • Fast Fresh Food • Fun Food for Children
Pasta • Fish and Shellfish • Mainly Vegetables • Meat and Poultry • Puddings
Best of British • Mediterranean Food • Tastes of the Orient

The Lifestyle Collection

Cooking for Health • Entertaining • The Essential Cookbook • Food for Friends